GOSPEL

JOURNAL

B&H
PUBLISHING GROUP
NASHVILLE, TENNESSEE

The Lord does not delay his promise, as some understand delay, but is patient with you, not wanting any to perish but all to come to repentance.
~2 Peter 3:9~